# EXCEPTIONAL ASIANS

# LAURENCE YEP

## Newbery Award-Winning Author

**Kristen Rajczak Nelson**

**Enslow Publishing**
101 W. 23rd Street
Suite 240
New York, NY 10011
USA

enslow.com

# Words to Know

**autobiography**—The life story of the person writing the book.

**aviator**—A person who flies planes or other aircraft.

**bilingual**—Involving the use of two languages.

**culture**—The beliefs, traditions, and habits of a group of people.

**generation**—A group of people born in the same general time period.

**immigrant**—Someone who travels to another country to live there.

**influenced**—Affected.

**journalism**—Writing done for magazines or newspapers.

**research**—The careful study of a topic.

# Contents

Laurence Yep

# CHAPTER 1

# Outside Two Worlds

**Laurence Yep** was born on June 14, 1948, in San Francisco, California. His grandfather on his father's side had been born in the same city in 1867, but Laurence's father was born in China and then returned to the United States. Laurence's mother was raised in West Virginia.

Laurence and his older brother Thomas lived with their parents in a mostly African American area of San Francisco. Their father owned a grocery store there, and the two boys had to work there whenever they could. Sometimes they started work as early as 6 AM !

## *Books as an Escape*

Being one of the only Chinese American children in a black area was made harder for Laurence because he didn't go to school with the other children in his neighborhood. Instead, he went to a Catholic school in Chinatown, a part of San Francisco that was mostly Chinese American. However, he felt like an outsider at school, too. It was a **bilingual** school, and Laurence barely spoke Chinese.

Laurence, age two, stands next to his father.

Laurence went to school in Chinatown, a part of San Francisco where many Chinese Americans live.

## Laurence Says:

"Science fiction and fantasy were about adapting, and that was something I did every day when I got on and off the bus."

Laurence learned that he could escape his feelings of being an outsider by reading fantasy and science fiction books. In books like *The Wizard of Oz*, characters were like Laurence—always having to learn to live in unfamiliar places and facing new situations. These books **influenced** Laurence's imagination and also comforted him.

# CHAPTER 2

# Discovering His Story

By the time Laurence was nearing the end of high school, he was mostly interested in science. He wanted to become a chemist. Then, an English teacher gave him a life-changing assignment. Laurence would only get an A in the class if he wrote a story for a national magazine and it was published. Though the teacher later

Laurence in his 1966 high school graduation portrait.

Laurence's first story was about an earthquake in San Francisco. There was a huge earthquake there in 1906.

changed the assignment to leave out the need for the story's acceptance, Laurence continued to try. He was rejected again and again—but that didn't stop him.

## Success!

Laurence started studying **journalism** at Marquette University in Wisconsin in 1966. Again, he felt like an outsider. There were few other Asian American students, and the weather was cold and snowy—nothing like San Francisco. Laurence was homesick and began writing about his home city. It turned into a story about San Francisco sinking into the ocean after an earthquake. The story sold, and Laurence was paid a penny a word. He was only eighteen!

## Laurence Says:

"All my science fiction stories, including that first one, were about alien creatures—or about alienated heroes. And I realized that in writing those stories I was really trying to work my way through to a clearer sense of who I was as a Chinese American."

Laurence became very interested in studying Chinese Americans and their history. This picture of a Chinese American family is from 1898.

Laurence finished college at the University of California, Santa Cruz, with a degree in literature. In his early twenties, Laurence gained a great interest in his family's roots and Chinese American **culture**. While studying Chinese American history, he found articles about a Chinese **aviator** from around 1900. This would be the basis of one of his most famous works, *Dragonwings*.

# CHAPTER 3

# Newbery Honoree

**In 1970,** Laurence published his first book for children. *Sweetwater* told the story of a boy named Tyree and his people trying to survive on a dangerous planet called Harmony. The book included both the science-fiction elements Laurence loved to read as a child as well as characters facing their world as outsiders. The book was just the beginning for Laurence as a children's author.

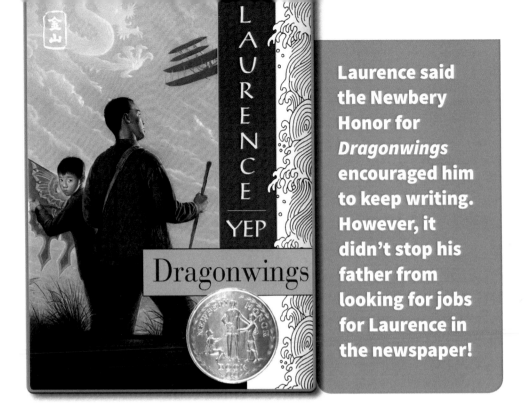

Laurence said the Newbery Honor for *Dragonwings* encouraged him to keep writing. However, it didn't stop his father from looking for jobs for Laurence in the newspaper!

### Dragonwings

Laurence finished his advanced degree in English literature in 1975. But perhaps the most exciting part of that year was the release of *Dragonwings*. The book told the story of an eight-year-old-boy traveling from China to San Francisco to be with his father in 1909. Laurence said that the story idea came from something he pictured in his mind: a plane flying over a hill. *Dragonwings* was popular. Laurence earned a Newbery Honor Medal for it!

*Dragonwings* clearly drew from Laurence's own past as a Chinese American child and the **research** he had done about Chinese American **immigrants**. When he was a child, there weren't many books about Chinese Americans, and those that he did find didn't seem real to him. As a writer, Laurence

## Laurence Says:

"Don't do it for the glory. Don't do it for the money, because most of the time it's not there . . . Even though I make a living at it, I'd be writing even if I was still bagging groceries in a grocery store."

Through his writing, Laurence honors the brave Chinese American immigrants of the past. The immigrants shown here arrived in California in the early 1900s.

has filled that hole for future Chinese American children by doing lots of research so that many of these books are based in history. Laurence is known for visiting small town libraries, constantly on the hunt for more stories about Chinese immigrants making their way in the United States.

# CHAPTER 4

# Writing What He Knows

**Laurence has** written more than sixty books, including another Newbery Honor book, *Dragon's Gate*. It is part of a series Laurence writes called the Golden Mountain Chronicles, which follows a Chinese American family through many **generations**. His books take place in many time periods and cross the globe—and beyond, such as *Sweetwater's* planet Harmony. In addition to books about Chinese culture, Laurence has written mysteries, plays, and even a *Star Trek* novel!

*The Lost Garden* tells the story of Laurence's early years and his struggle to find his place in the world.

## Connecting to Culture

Laurence has said that Chinese culture is what he knows about, so that's what he writes. He encourages young writers to do the same. Laurence has talked to writing classes of many ages, and he has taught at the University of California.

## Laurence Says:

"Children sometimes think you have to have special experiences to write, but good writing brings out what's special in ordinary things."

Laurence believes that young people can write if they just open themselves up to the world around them.

To his students, Laurence says: "Writing only requires taking one step to the side and looking at something from a slightly different angle."

In 1991, Laurence published an **autobiography** called *The Lost Garden*. In it Laurence writes about his background and how writing helped him overcome feeling like an outsider. The special background that he describes in *The Lost Garden* has surely influenced Laurence's writing and encouraged his great imagination. But he has said young writers don't need more than their daily life and imagination to write from: "I really think it's part of just being open to the world. We learn to shut ourselves off from our feelings and memories, and a writer learns how to connect all those things together."

# Timeline

**1948**—Laurence Yep is born on June 14.

**1966**—Graduates from high school.

**1969**—"Selchy Kids," the first story Laurence ever sold, is included in *World's Best Science Fiction of 1969*.

**1970**—Earns degree from the University of California, Santa Cruz.

**1973**—Publishes first book, *Sweetwater*.

**1975**—Finishes doctoral degree in English literature at the State University of New York at Buffalo.

**1975**—*Dragonwings* is named a Newbery Medal Honor Book.

**1991**—Publishes autobiography, *The Lost Garden*.

**1994**—Receives second Newbery Honor with *Dragon's Gate*.

**2005**—Awarded the Laura Ingalls Wilder Medal for his contribution to children's literature.

**2011**—Publishes *Dragons of Silk*, the conclusion to *Dragonwings* and *Dragon's Gate*.

# Learn More

## Books

Ehrlich, Amy, ed. *When I Was Your Age: Original Stories About Growing Up*. Somerville, MA: Candlewick Press, 2012.

Kingston, Anna. *Respecting the Contributions of Asian Americans*. New York: PowerKids Press, 2012.

Wilson, Steve. *The California Gold Rush: Chinese Laborers in America (1848–1882)*. New York: PowerKids Press, 2016.

Yep, Laurence, and Joanne Ryder. *A Dragon's Guide to the Care and Feeding of Humans*. New York: Crown Books for Young Readers, 2015.

## Websites

eduplace.com/kids/hmr/mtai/yep.html
Find out more about Laurence Yep as well as a short list of books he has written.

encyclopedia.kids.net.au/page/li/List_of_famous_Chinese_Americans
Discover more about other notable Chinese Americans.

readingrockets.org/books/interviews/yep
Watch a video interview with Laurence Yep and find out more about his writing.

# Index

Published in 2017 by Enslow Publishing, LLC.
101 W. 23rd Street, Suite 240, New York, NY 10011

**Library of Congress Cataloging-in-Publication Data**
Names: Nelson, Kristen Rajczak, author.
Title: Laurence Yep : Newbery Award-winning author /
Kristen Rajczak Nelson.
Description: New York, NY : Enslow Publishing, 2017.
| Series: Exceptional Asians | Includes bibliographical
references and index.
Identifiers: LCCN 2015044481| ISBN 9780766078390
(library bound) | ISBN 9780766078451 (pbk.) | ISBN
9780766078055 (6-pack)
Subjects: LCSH: Yep, Laurence--Juvenile literature. |
Authors, American--20th century--Biography--Juvenile
literature. | Young adult fiction--Authorship--Juvenile
literature. | Chinese Americans--Biography--Juvenile
literature.
Classification: LCC PS3575.E6 Z85 2016 | DDC 813/.54--dc23
LC record available at http://lccn.loc.gov/2015044481

Printed in Malaysia

**To Our Readers:** We have done our best to make
sure all website addresses in this book were active
and appropriate when we went to press. However,
the author and the publisher have no control over
and assume no liability for the material available on
those websites or on any websites they may link to.
Any comments or suggestions can be sent by e-mail to
customerservice@enslow.com.

**Photo Credits**: Throughout book, ©Toria/Shutterstock.
com (blue background); cover, pp. 1, 4, 20 Joanna
Ryder; p. 4 Paul Morigi/Getty Images for Ovation; pp.
6, 9 Courtesy Laurence Yep; p. 7 ullstein bild via Getty
Images; p. 10 National Archives/Wikimedia Commons/
San Francisco Earthquake of 1906, (This is an) area
is possibly in the vicinity of Bush and Battery Streets
- NARA - 531042.tif/ public domain; p. 12 Universal
History Archive/UIG via Getty Images; p. 14 © 2001 by
Tim O'Brien/Cover © 2001 by HarperCollins Publishers
Inc.; p. 16 FPG/Getty Images; p. 18 photo taken by
Megan Quick.